To dear John.
All my love Marie X

C000296675

THE BREATHING EARTH

David Austin

THE BREATHING
EARTH

First published in 2014
by Enitharmon Press
10 Bury Place
London WC1A 2JL

www.enitharmon.co.uk

Distributed in the UK by
Central Books
99 Wallis Road
London E9 5LN

ISBN: 978-1-907587-96-2 (hardback)
ISBN: 978-1-907587-75-7 (paperback)

Enitharmon Press gratefully acknowledges the financial support of
Arts Council England through Grants for the Arts.

British Library Cataloguing-in-Publication Data.
A catalogue record for this book is available
from the British Library.

Designed in Albertina by Libanus Press
and printed in England by
CPI Antony Rowe Ltd

CONTENTS

THE BREATHING EARTH

The breathing earth is mad for life.
By growth, by struggle and by strife,
it tramples on the frail and weak.
The brave and strong it always seeks

And yet to man is kind and good,
bird and beast and flower and sod.
It seeks for blood that we may prove
the spirit and the power of love.

The spark is lit at frailest birth,
seed of love is born of earth,
when a mother first holds her child,
she feels the message of the wild.

SOME CASUAL PASSER-BY

Soon we both shall share a stone
that will for ever be our own,
though centuries shall pass us by:
there we, peacefully, shall lie.

And, when at last we have returned to clay,
perhaps some casual passer-by will say,
'These two, once, did have their day.'
And yet, in truth, he will not know
the joy we did together know.

THE PARTING

A man leans from the window of a departing train;
a woman with her children waves goodbye.
She has a vigour that stands out from the crowd
like the bright centre of a painting.

They are drawn together as they part,
and yet they part, as all one day must.
Soon he is gone, and she turns for home.
The wire is cut, the light is out –
the life has gone from the platform.

He will remember this scene
over the long years of his life:
her light –
and the sparkling innocence of their children.

AUTUMN WALK

These are the quiet days of autumn
that already hold the spring in their lap:
the leaves brown upon the ground,
the grass heavy with moisture,
the young winter wheat.
Contentment – poet,
have we no words for this?

Had I a few acres
I think I might find religion in a crop of corn –
I might see a permanence in this.
This is a day to remember,
set between the collapsing of two storms,
like the penetrating of pain,
to find the good within.

This wooded valley impedes me joyfully:
there is much life in a few steps of damp earth;
the adding up of mud on the boots is a pleasant labour.

Where am I going?
Through the field gates of time?
Why must man breathe so heavily upon the world?
I will ride upon these banks:
plainly there are more depths than these.
How often have I been here, and seen nothing?

Who needs to believe?
We *are* – this is belief.
I have come through much pain to this.

Can we speak of completion?
I think not.
Come, you careful ones,
I know there is reason in it.
Do I speak plainly?

The words have made these thoughts for me –
I speak for my own understanding:
poems cannot but tell truth.

My boots have washed in the stream –
my mind also.
That bird's nest is broken –
God has spoken.

I turn for home.
There are more finches on a fair day.
This is a struggle – I know that.

GORILLA

There was a gorilla at the zoo –
a rather clever fellow, too.
He studied men of many kinds,
amazing the world with his finds.

He kept his humans in a cage,
writing notes, page by page.
He would give them motor cars,
and they would play with them for hours.

At six o'clock he'd give them tea –
just like gorillas do, you see.
Then with his friends he'd make a bet:
'They'll watch the television set.'

Then he would close a little door
so they'd not see it any more.
See how they'd rant and how they'd roar,
and roll in rage upon the floor.

Though at times they seemed quite kind,
all at once they change their mind,
and bash each other on the head.
They'd sometimes do it till they were dead.

This habit he could not explain –
it puzzled his gorilla brain.

THE CITY OF LOST BELIEF

When the first non-believer came to town
they built a fire and burned him down.
They threw his body in a well,
and left him then to rot in Hell.

When the last non-believer came
they built a throne
And on his head they placed a crown.
The people sighed in their relief
from the burden of belief.

The word went round, 'The people die –
the temple god has lost his eye.'
Into the town there came a clown,
and on his head they placed the crown.
See how these stones are strewn around!

BIRTH

When the breath came to the newly living,
songs of battle sweet it sung:
a body bearing a soul away
had been born upon this day.

In the wilderness of war
it had never been before.
In the madness of creation –
A heart beats that did not beat before.

THE HILL'S MOODS

To lie once more beside this hill,
and hear the curlews crying still,
though they may cry for fear of ill,
does with peace my body fill.

The vixen basking with her cubs
gives no hint of fearful jaw,
until tensed for blood once more
she paces forth on silent paw.

Men have fought upon this hill,
their hearts each other out to kill.
This cruel hill is bleak and cold –
a challenge only for the bold

Yes, men have died upon this hill:
for all I know, they lie here still.
Their blood and bones sweet flowers do fill –
for all I know.

The heather on the hillside rides –
its roots are tethered to her side.
Though wind may cry from troubled skies,
no care, nor succour, she denies.

This hill is mother to the grass,
this gentle hill is soft and still –
all woman to the world beneath:
all kinds of life on her I find.

Bird and beast and flower and leaf –
all life does nestle in her breast.
I think I'll lay me here and rest:
this gentle hill is quiet and still.

Oh gentle hill, you're strong and kind,
a place to run to and to hide.
Inside your growth I'm lost from view
I think I'll lie awhile with you.

GOD GAVE MAN THOUGHT

And God gave man thought.
And the man stood and thought

And he thought –
some became plants,
some became trees,
some became fishes,
some became beasts,
and some became men.

And all fought –
and some conquered,
and some gave,
and there was joy, and pain.

And the man laughed, and cried,
and was filled with ecstasy –
for what he saw
was too beautiful, and cruel, to bear.
And the wind blew across the earth,
And scattered his dust in its crevices.

And the man, so thinking,
took his loved one in his arms,
and kissed her,
and held his children high to the sky,
in laughter, and in love,
and thought of some small good deed,
and went about his work, in happiness.

GIVING UP

The fire is burning in me still,
but now it flames against my will.
I would like to damp it down –
act the fool, or play the clown,
and warm myself against the end,
for no man can his life extend:
that which is past we cannot mend;
who has no faith had best pretend.

There is not much I wish to do
except to sit and watch
the television programme.

Let those who will
go out and fight
or bed a lovely lover.
If you don't mind
I'll just sit here
and leave that to you, my brother.

I have, like you, but these few years –
a sojourn in this vale of tears.
I do not see in myself might –
I will not scale the dizzy height.
I'll shed my load, and travel light.
I do not see myself as such,
I do not see myself as much:
I see myself as very small.

God Almighty, save us all!

GREAT MAN

There once was a famous hero,
who would always fight for the right,
whenever there was an evil,
he'd be in the thick of the fight.

And he was like a beacon,
that shone with a blaze of light.
But only God knows our true soul,
as we sleep with our dreams at night.

One day there came a telephone call,
from his wild and distraught wife.
It seemed their son had tried
to put an end to his life.

So he rang up his solicitor –
a clever and resourceful man –
and told him, 'John is being difficult,' –
how he had tried to put an end to his life –
'Please do what you can.'

For he was engaged in great issues,
and he was a busy man,
and he must be like a beacon,
that shines with a blaze of light.

But only God knows our true soul,
as we sleep with our dreams at night.

A NEWBORN CHILD

A little lume of light –
a light to pierce the night –
a cry to rend the heavens –
a joy on earth and heaven –
a strong, but frail thing:

a little newborn child!

CHILDREN

Little beings –
small dawning spirits
full of curiosity and delight
already struggle for the light.

They are looking through a small window
upon a new world.
Consciousness is come upon them
like a new day creeping over hills.

How we love them!
We would smother them with our love.
But we must not –
for they have their own small souls to tend.

LITTLE CHILD

We laugh to see him laugh;
we are sad to see him cry;
we hold his tiny hands;
we kiss his little head;
we dance him on our knees,
and sing him little songs;
we love to see him play;
we hold him up to walk,
and point him to the world:
we have such love for him
as he can never know.

But time will surely come
when we must let him go
upon his own brief way.

AN IMPORTANT PERSON

Do not much heed what they say,
for today they will say this,
and tomorrow will say that,
and the next they will wash it all away,
and start all over again –
for newspapers must be sold,
politicians elected,
and experts cannot be without something to offer.

The knowledgeable like to be knowledgeable,
and the clever, clever.
The reasonable man has worked it all out,
and the women knew it all the time in their bones.
Beneath all this, human nature remains
much as it always was:
we are born, breathe, eat, make love, and must die –
as we always have.

Our joys and sorrows remain unchanged –
the evil done a thousand years ago
we still understand today –
only too well.
The battles fought then
must be fought all over again.
'Only love shall make us whole' –
that, at least, is true.

But what is there that we should do?
Let us summon all women great with child
and those with toddlers at their feet,
and tell them how it is
that through them alone, we are complete.

Not the bustle of the street,
not the rich, and not the poor,
not the brave, and not the good,
not the sun, nor the bright fresh air,
not the teacher, nor the priest,
but she with children at her feet
must do the job for all the rest.

THE SWIMMER

Deep and blue,
deep and blue –
went down to the crystal sea,
and the fishes there
do dart and leap,
and never thought me a foe.

Crystal water, cool and free
always you are good to me.
Though I wrestle with your strength
muscles striving all my length,
though you send a cruel wave,
still I'll be a willing slave.

Like a seal I slip inside
through your calmest deep to glide,
coming up for living air
that I may my strength repair.
Floating, weaving, diving, dipping,
like a fish – silent, slipping
far away from safety's shore,
I, your distant caves explore.

There I'm poised like bird on air
down in clearest deep I stare.
Previous life is hanging here
fraught with a delicious fear.

My heart beats like a bat;
my lungs pump like a bellow.
All my body an engine –
only my mind sitting and seeing,
holding the whole on a rein,
urging on, ignoring fatigue –
a master beating his slave.

I hold up my life with my will,
my body soaked in the sunlight,
the sunlight soaked in the sea.
I am a feather sailing a pool –
a speck that is lost in the distance –
of importance to no-one but me.

THE BEAUTIFUL

Some may say we're silly,
and more would say we're bad.
Some may be pleased to see us fall,
and a few, perchance, be sad.
But all will know our little sin –
'e'er all is said and done',
but only you and I, my dear, can know –
'e'er all is done and said' –
that we are beautiful in bed.

TRUST

To I, who was a woman waiting,
he came to me out of a dream kingdom,
believing in my life-giving,
praising the joy in me.

I, who rated myself lowly,
he bore me unto believing,
believing in my soul's clarity
and body's bare beauty,
seeing me not in my true reality,
until I became as he saw me,
all life lovely, my eyes speaking truly
of what I never knew was in me,
saying – 'My burden of life I bring to you:
take it, it is all for you.
These are my small pleasures –
take them – they are all for you.
Make what you will of them –
I trust you.'

So it was I took his belief,
and my whole self gave,
though I lived for a world and a day –
I will be wife to him.

LIFE

Kiss a little,
love a little,
with your body
bless a little.

Laugh a little,
cry a little:
every day
we die a little.

OUT OF THIS LOVE

Out of this love
the light arises.
Energy blossoms into meaning:
people dance and sing,
flowers bloom,
and fields and hills have life.

So spirit flowers,
and God is known;
and blessedness is born –
and love – in all its forms.

TOGETHER

Two men sort through a hill of sand
to find a little speck of gold,
and when this speck one did behold
he gave it to his friend,
who put it back into the sand
that they might seek it all again.

Now what they'd lost they both do share,
and they will never be alone.

THE FLOWERS

The flowers, the flowers!
They are so violent –
their energy overwhelms us.

They will not let us rest.
What do they know of tragedy?
Their short days pass in happiness.
Their small hurts barely touch them.
June is theirs.

Their joy is so infectious
it fills our hearts with hope.
We gather them into our arms
that we may share their life.

They dance in the wind –
into the future they go,
leaving a little happiness.

Come with me into the garden,
and I will show you!

Snowdrop

Here is a mystery:
this little snowdrop
that strives in the early year
for its first glimpse of the sun,
out of the great burden of the earth.

The blood, too, is like this,
surging in the veins,
fighting to show the world
its short moment of beauty

Both sing their little songs,
beautiful and sad.
The same power moves both:
what this is we do not know.

Primroses

Here are the primroses.
They are little children
in the spring of their lives

Their innocence is such
that we cannot tell them.

Let us pick some,
and make a posy –
that we may never lose hope.

Daffodils

The daffodils are
simple country women
in yellow bonnets.

They are so dependable:
what would we do without them?

Every spring they come,
with chattering conversation.

They dance plain country dances –
their faces beam innocent joy.

They know exactly where they stand:
they have such senses of right.

You may be sure
they will be here again next year.

Cherry Blossom

The cherry blossom is here,
but only for the day.

Their rosy cheeks
and dappling dresses
delight us all.

See how they dance!
And the sky –
it is clear blue behind them!

Oh – we are so happy!

Tulips

The tulips –
they are so immaculate!

Nothing of theirs is ever out of place;
they are always perfect:
they can never be wrong.

If they were – just sometimes –
I am sure we would love them more.

Although they put on a brave show,
I notice they go inside for the winter.

Irises

The irises are out in the garden.
In their silken rainbow dresses
they are so colourful,
so brilliant and so clever.
They talk incessantly.

Everyone admires them –
they demand that we should.

You cannot ignore them.
But what are they really like?

Roses

Here are the roses
that know all about people,
and yet are still filled with love.

True, they have thorns that tear.
But we forgive them
for their lovely humanity.

They suit us:
they have lived with us so long.

When the others have gone
they will still be here,
sending up strong, sustaining branches
through the thicket of our lives.

They are familiar faces:
they give us a sense of security.

Lilies

How calm are the lilies,
all in purest white!

They are like untouched brides,
or nuns of perfect purity.
Their innocence is not human:

they are goddesses
of mystic virtue.

They outshine all the rest.
But who would dare to touch them?

Orchids

These are the orchids.
They believe in the jungle.

They do not believe in virtue.
They are much too sophisticated –
and so expensive.

They are most at home
on the breasts of cold women.

We admire them –
but we will never truly love them.

Michaelmas Daisies

The Michaelmas Daisies have come at last.
They are so wise:
they have seen it all –
how the flowers come and go,
and never remain.

They have a kind of mellow contentment,
I think, in their hearts:
they are truly happy,
for they have accepted the world
as it is.

INCOMPATIBLE

We cannot live with a lie:
I have fields so bleak and so high
that she is unable to climb,
and hers, though so lush, and so deep,
run nowhere near mine.

For I am a lover of hills,
and the thrills of the climb,
and distances deeper than time.
But she is a picker of flowers,
and her path leads nowhere near mine.

MURRELL'S WOOD

This is another valley,
sadder than the last,
where the trees stretch up their arms for light,
and all in darkest beauty fight.

Beneath these trees all is night,
and rotting trunks once strong with growth
soon fall and decay,
while the water in the trickling stream,
unconscious of the pain of life,
goes laughing on its way,
in mineral ecstasy.

AUTUMN

The passing of a passing year
lies in the loam of rotting leaves.
In the falling of a falling leaf
there's but a moment for its grief,
for always shoots arise again
as, ever fleeting in the brain,
so hopes,
so fears,
so joys,
so tears.

WINTER TREES

See the bare arms of the trees!
Ah, it is good that it is winter,
and all the fuss and struggle of leaves is over,
and we may step into the anonymity of winter.

It is good that it is winter,
and the trees are stripped of all the nonsense of leaves,
as one who has shed the pretentions of clothes
is bare unto the soul.

NEW YEAR'S EVE

The leaves have gone from the trees.
The plants rest in the warm earth.
The trees wait, tall and bare,
the wind in their upper branches,
while beneath, all is still and quiet.

There is a peace in this lack of life,
like the stillness of a silent god.
There is no struggle,
life rests,
I will wait here
while my mind unwinds
the trauma of a torn year.

WINTER

She is like the winter:
you cannot tell
if love can be found
under the frozen soil.

Only I know:
she does not say,
or touch, or feel, or kiss.

She shows only
the stern exterior of reason:
she is so unreasonable.

I suppose in the last reaches of winter
we shall all be swallowed up,
and it will not matter any more.

But I remember the flowers and love of spring.
Now I wonder, did it ever happen?

REASON AND EMOTION

He had a theory in his mind –
a reason to be so unkind.

Reason builds and builds and builds,
and reinforces ancient ills.

While emotion swells and easily dies,
and sun returns, and clear skies.

PROGRESS

They made a new machine
that could out-think the human brain,
and everything explain.

They feared this mad machine –
they feared its dreadful brain.
For no machine can love,
and no machine can hate,
and no machine can know
the pain of human plight,
or fight the human fight,
or know the sweet delight
of lips on honey lips.

For this is simple truth
that man is human breath,
and man is human flesh,
and he can soon be tired,
and often he's afraid,
and with a simple blow
he can be destroyed.

His desire it is to live –
his need it is to love –
and that he should be loved.
He lives by good and evil,
God's creation to unravel.
He lives by what he has not,
and not by what he's got.

A FLOWER OF THE HIMALAYAS

A flower of the Himalayas
on this Welsh hillside, says its prayers.
A flower from another land
is trying to make us understand.
Its prayers, though they be Hindu
are yet the same,
for me and you.

BETRAYAL

They stood together, at my door,
these men I had known from the start,
and struck a coldness in my heart,
for men together can do great good or ill
and men together are not as men apart.

'We are sorry,' they said,
these men I had known from the start.
'And yet, it has to be said,' they said,
'and while we do not wish you harm,
we have a duty to perform.'

For men who have said one thing to your face
and say quite another, in another place –
and men together are not as men apart.

THE BROKEN SOCIETY

We think we are alone,
and deserted by the pack.
We are conscious of the load of guilt
that we carry on our back.

We think we are unworthy,
and that none will let us in.
What we can not know, of course,
is that the pack has been dispersed,
and the others, too, are crying,
and fearing for the worst.

Here is the reason modern man
is said to be accursed.
Yet this is how the song of man
has been blazed across the sky,
for he who has the wish to live
must be prepared to die,
and only he who's tasted ill
can know when all is well,
and first we each must go away
if we are ever to come back.

TOMB ROBBERS

In the filching of an ancient temple tomb, they tore
at the half-buried mantle of a long-decaying door,
until at last, peering inside, half dismayed, they saw
shining idols more ancient far than were their own,
and around this glittering store were strewn
the remnants of many a human bone,
where ancient men were peaceful, laid to rest,
safe in the knowledge that they at least were blessed.

At the sight of which the robbers cried unto their Gods,
'Explain! Explain!'
And from the depths of the tomb they heard a voice reply,
'Hear me. I was here before all this began.
I have been here while all these gods have come and gone.
It was I to whom they prayed,
who once did pray unto this store of gold.
It was I in whom he lost his faith,
who last did close this door.
I was their God then, and shall be evermore.
But they who scoff, how shall they pray?
Who have Gods not idols gilt in gold?
How shall they my eternal truth behold?'

THE DISILLUSIONED

Only a few words between us two
that once were all living flesh and pastures new.
Out of all this joy and pleasure
we are left with this –
a carefully measured measure.

How can sadness come from so high a hope?
How can pain pursue so sweet a pleasure?
Yet still our war grinds on,
though both may wish it other,
for love and hate were ever lovers' lover.

A FADING STAR

I girdle the earth without knowing,
I search in the sky without finding,
I am lost in the mystery of being:
here, I am but the last of the past,
a creature that hasn't a future.

Here I have not a purpose but being –
perhaps this is the profoundest of seeing.
O fear, do not fear for your safety,
O mind, do not mind if you're lost,
O care, do not care for your caring,
for mystery's the best of our being.

We must pay for a song with a sorrow;
we must pay for a joy with a tear.
My mind has no room for tomorrow;
my soul has no place for a fear.

I have come to the crux of the question
and I know that my end must be near.
I am nought but a star that is failing –
floating in space like a dream –
for this is the song I must sing.

PROVERBS

What is there that we can say
to help the sad man on his way?
The road to truth is long and rough:
we know too much, yet not enough.

And who is there this truth to teach?
We reach and reach, yet cannot reach.
If we should, we search our minds for ever:
the clever may not be so clever.

Some overcome their fears with mirth,
and do not have to face the truth,
or cultivate a piece of land,
and do not try to understand.

Some say they do not know or care,
and so dispose of their despair.
He who counts the days to come
may make a sadness of his sum.

A warning to the pat believer –
the mind was ever a deceiver.
That which was true but yesterday
may prove an illusion by today.
Yet we who live and soon must die
would like to know the reason why.
How strange to know, then simply die
How did we come to have our say?

How is it that we care so much?
Why do we cling to our belief?
Perhaps it is we need such pain
with which to cultivate the brain.

Who'd find the precious source of life
must take the fearful road of strife.
As in a play we should be glad:
much sadness is not to be sad.

For still the dance of life is sweet,
as dancers find on dancing feet.
Who feels a song inside them sing
to this small evidence should cling.

He who looks upon a flower
may sense a deep, elusive power.
Who has the chance to share a task
no further happiness need ask.

He who takes to him a friend
most human sadnesses can mend.
Who learns of God has found a grace
that all the world will put in place.

A COLD WIND COMING

You, who have torn my body,
am I no more singular to you?
You, who have torn my soul,
am I no more your one love-making?

I feel a cold wind coming,
and my womb withers in the waiting.
Why do you come no more to me?
All my pleasures I store for you.
Are my joys no more joy-making?

Here I lie, unsleeping
fearful of waking.
Oh, that the earth would swallow,
and take me!

LOVE'S DOWNWARD SPIRAL

They had a row –
well, lovers do.
They had another –
that's not so bad.
They had another and another –
and many, many more.

Then they began to see
that they were living on love's capital.
Fear crept in –
and fear fed on fear.

But still they'd not give in:
it was love's downward spiral,
and they were caught within.

SCORNED

I am bitter in my bare bed.
I am bitter for all the bitterness in my head.
I, who gave you my garden and orchard,
and myself, to be a house for you
am bitter, with a bitter hatred.

So I am burning my belief now,
and selling myself to the best bidder.
For you, who would have me,
though all the world said, 'No,'
now no more care whether I come or go.

Care not, for I am going,
for I well know, there is nothing.
What have I been doing with you these years,
oh you, that I do not trust?

What have I been doing in your arms,
oh you, that I do not know?
You came to me from nowhere,
you came out of the mist.

Oh, why do I wish to lay my head
on your cold, unfeeling breast?
All of life's a mystery;
all of life's a jest.

Why do I wish to lay my head
on your cold, unfeeling breast?

The wheels of time grind in our heads:
they grind our love to dust.
So – what am I doing here with you,
oh, you that I do not trust?

MEGALOMANIA

Here is a great growth
that darkens all light,
permitting no life,
having not knowledge nor reason,
knowing not good nor bad,
willing only what it wishes,
caring nothing,

Yet ever growing.
This great growth
has long, strong tendrils
with which it strangles all its fellows.

THE MAD LOVER

In waves of hatred for her love
she moves back and across –
now in the land of living,
now in a sea of dross.

And yet each night within their bed
they hold a joyful mass.
But still she hates the one she loves,
and loves the one she hates,
and washes her hair in dark despair,
combs it out in pain,
as it grows upon her lovely head
out of her tangled brain.

REMEMBRANCE DAY

I

Twelve scarlet soldiers marching,
drums fiercely beating;
a hundred veterans walking,
medals brightly shining,
some in bowlers important-looking;
others with round shoulders, hiding;
ten nurses rambling;
Boy Scouts stride, determined-looking;
Girl Guides tripping;
parents laughing;
parson with his choirboys, waiting;
everywhere people looking:
so much emotion,
as in the weekday streets
familiar faces meet,
until, in the sunlit square,
all are gathered there,
for silence, and prayer.

II

See the soldiers marching:
their drummers seem to say,
We are marching here for England,
and innocence today.
We all know about selfishness –
the crude and the dull.
But innocence and England
must also have their say.
The people here are happy
when perhaps they should be sad.
But if the dead men could see them
I think they would be glad.

HAPPINESS REMEMBERED

What was it that she brought?
What was it that she had?
Did she sizzle in the sack?
Was she best upon her back?

O, this I can't deny –
I remember with a sigh –
no, it was the sweet content
of those years we spent.

It was the human worth
that her clever presence brought.
It was when we were together
that we never were alone.

O I have written poetry,
and many songs have sung
since all the world was shining youth,
and you and I were young.

And sometimes they were happy,
and sometimes they were sad
but there's not been a song I've sung
without you being there,
and maybe they'll be sung again,
and maybe they'll be lost.

But many more will pass this way
where we were tempest-tossed;
and many more will sing their songs,
and many more will die,
and many more together lie,
when we together lie.

SYMPATHY

Blessed balm of sympathy,
soothing all our ills.
Loving care in kindness
hole of sorrow fills.

So we are not lonely,
so we are not sad,
and thus our little troubles
do not seem so bad.

Who has soul of sympathy
for a gift to give
has the loving essence:
power to make us live.

bringing growth of courage
more powerful than war.
Such a deep vitality
does our life restore.

DESPAIR

I am a fragment of the universe:
I am fragmented.
There are places in my mind
where neither God nor loved one ever went.

I consort with myself alone,
alone among misty people.
My mind is like a barren world
whose sun arises in a lazy dream.

I have forgotten what was in me once
of love and life, and deep belief.
The watery sun sees through the autumn trees:
I see my lost beliefs like fallen leaves.

FRAGMENTS FROM A FUNERAL

I

A peculiar invention is Man,
who does as nothing else can,
who lives with his soul,
like a rat in a hole,
then lies down and dies like a lamb.

II

So practical,
so practical
so practical we must be
when she has died.

We most did love
first bury her, say we.
Then we will cry
our lonely tears,
and no-one else shall see.

III

The hand that held her dying hand
to comfort her
now feels another hand
to comfort it.
Is it not good that sadness is so kind?
I feel the warmth of love grow in my mind.

IV

Beneath this stone
two lovers lie,
the grass a quilt,
the soil a bed,
close when they lived –
close now they're dead.

V

Squatting in a tearful crouch
she stumbles like a wounded bird
to read the lovely wreaths of flowers
upon her mother's grave.

VI

This house is waiting to die.
Soon it will cease to be.
The woman that it was
they will take apart
limb by limb,
and tear out its heart,
and it will become someone else.

AFTER THE FUNERAL

The mind has cleared,
the pain is gone,
the sun does shine –
and we live on.

The breath of spring
has touched the grass,
and in the blood
is its fighting blast.

A joy to find
in the solitary mind –
a community of another kind
that jostles and fights,
and loves through the nights,
and talks and laughs,
with the blood so red
that bubbles and bursts
from heart to head,
and has no thought
for the long-time dead –
and has no thought
for the long-time dead.

LOSS

We took her to the gates of time,
beyond all reason and all rhyme,
and in sadness left her there,
beyond the boundary of our care.
Further thought, we did not dare,
and yet she had walked without a fear.
So it was we came
to the last confusion,
which is death.
Oh, how shall we show grief
that have no form for it?
No plans were laid – no long farewell –
no thought of either Heaven or Hell
No solemn feast – no mumbling priest –
no message for the broken-hearted:
just – unceremoniously – departed.
Four men came to fetch my love
that I once called 'my swirly dove',
in a big black car to take her away
in the bright light of a fresh May day.
They took her and placed her underground,
where now she lies without a sound.
I did not know until she'd gone away
all that she had been to me.
And now at night I lie alone
upon my stony bed,
with all my sorrows in my arms,
and terror in my head.
It seemed our lives
had both been planned
before our day of birth.
It seemed that we were puppets, strung,
or actors in a play
For life is short –
I'll tell you now –
and it's a tragedy.

DREAM

A poet dreamed a dream:
his life became a song.
In this he found a friend –
a kind of demon god,
who took him by the hand,
and would not let him go –
who showed him mysterious things
he had never thought to see –
made him bigger and more bold
than he ever thought to be.

But only in the song
was the mystery revealed:
it was like being in love –

a sort of painful joy
that seldom brought content.
It, like unto a fight
that might either end in death
or a terrible delight.

They roamed in many lands,
where he had never thought to go.
They walked on morning dew,
where everything was fresh,
and everything was new.

First they met a heathen priest
who could talk direct to God,
who could say that this was good,
or could say that that was bad,
who would slash, with knives, his breast,
to be a lesson to the rest,

or lie prostrate in the dust.
To a god, who said he must –
to be worthy of his trust.

Next, dusky, darkling girls
offered sensuous love to him,
telling of the charms
in their cool encircling arms,
and of the juicy fruit
that they had held within.

One tempted him to her,
showed him ancient joys
that she had there for him,
whose love was like a heaven
that he could hardly bear –
an ecstasy and fire
that went beyond desire –
a heaven in a heaven,
a fire within a fire,
a confined and human place:
a state of human grace.

Onward then to war,
blood pulsing on before
to the glory of a fight
that might well end in night.
A fearful human rite
where one man must lie dead
to salve another's pride;
saw a bride all dressed in black
for a man who wouldn't come back
because he loved a whore:
the sad instinct for war;

the bleak beauty of the blood;
the live man, and the dead;
a narrow channel where
a man must meet despair.

Then back into the past,
musing, 'Nothing here will last,'
to a heap of crumbling stones,
and long-decaying bones
that once did lie in love,
with those vaulted in stone above,
to a dark and fearful land –
a land of long decay –
a land of the unknown,
of the soil amongst the bones
where in the end we all must go.

There were times when the dream
like a comic strip did seem –
Man's stupidity and folly
seemed to make him almost merry.
At his lying and his pride
they would almost burst his sides,
laughing at his petty fears
that they might hold back the tears.
Yet more often they were happy
than ever they were sad,
for more often they saw good
than ever they saw bad,
seeing joy come out of tears,
and courage out of fears.

It was often in the fields
that their song would be revealed,
singing in the breeze
that was playing in the trees,

leading them along
in an ecstasy of song
to a place of perfect peace
where the earth could catch her breath
lying stretched out in her dress
in her lovely, flowery dress
where the mind could be at peace,
and love could have its say,
be it only for the day.

Sometimes in the mind
they would be confined
trying to understand the riddle
that's the spirit of mankind –
the mystery that is breath –
the nonsense that is death:
all the joy, and all the trouble,
whose end is like a bubble.

Through the mysteries of time,
through the mysteries of space,
blindfolded they paced
in search of the divine –
to make complete their rhyme.

What they sought was a control
that would make their song a whole –
a precise and rhythmic beat,
out of chaos and defeat –
a song to defeat death,
the heartbeat and the breath;
a passionate expanse
made into a rhythmic dance;
a blow that's full of power,
with a poise that's like a flower,
and as gentle as a flower,

making beauty of the pain
that is lodged within the brain;
an energy that comes
from the very roots of life,
like a dancer in a trance,
who must dance, and dance, and dance,
until his last heartbeat is spent,
like a lover with his love,
in a love that never ends.

TWO TRUTHS

I know people who pale at the question.
I know others who will not give in.
But some must lose out in the struggle:
there are those who must lose if we win;
there are those who think kindness a weakness,
while others think love is a sin.

A tear's no sure sign of sorrow:
pain may be masked by a smile.
You can ask if you can think of the question:
you'll not know if you do find the answer.
Yet each life is the birth of a nation:
a war we can lose or can win.

At the end you will find there's a mystery:
there are but two truths I can tell you –
fear is the thing that is fatal,
and love is the only reality.

MADMAN

A madman sang for sixpence
to an audience that was not there,
with all the angels in Heaven
beneath the thatch of his hair.
For what he saw was a glory,
while all we saw was despair.

And I wondered,
is it better be a madman happy,
or is it better be a sane man sad?
Could all the angels in Heaven
ever make us so glad?

BEING

I speak upon the edge of time –
make a few words rhyme –
for there's reason in a small compass,
and pleasure in the pain of knowing.

I am the last of a lovely day,
hung upon the brink of being,
appalled in its glory,
knowing not how, nor why, but am.

Life bursts for me:
strength is a strong glory.
O, hollow eyes of Time,
wait a little for me!

MOTHER AND CHILD

Baby nestling at the breast –
what importance here is pressed!
What a rage, and what a fire!
What a havoc could transpire!

Lady with the milky breast,
what is it here he does digest?
Know you in this milk he'll find
all the sorrows of mankind?

No, lady, do not think this so.
Out of you he will well know
all the love that you have fed
is stored within his little head.

From the thrilling of your soul
this is how he will be whole.
Lady with the milky breast,
out of you he will be blessed.

THE SEA BY MOONLIGHT

Sleepless I lie
the long night through.

In the distance,
the whispering of the sea,
in which we were
but this afternoon –
like two fishes.

No, the sea does not give up.
Her restless body moves,
even in the night,
while the clear-faced moon –
her lover –
sparkles in her belly,
and the land lies still in sleep.

HANDS

Nature extending from the brain
invented the beauty of hands
that have such power to do and touch,
and without words can say so much.

Your hands came to me
like messengers of love,
like little leaves
to touch my soul,
and spoke such words
as no words could.

And what they said,
was happiness and good.
As we hold hands
the power runs through,
from you to me,
and me to you.

'Hold out your hands to me today,
and with our hands we everything will say.'

WIFE

My little busy bee;
my little housemaid, free;
my cleaner of nooks and crannies;
my children's friend;
my minder and my mind;
my cultivator, cook and kindly one;
my stitcher, polisher, painter, artist, friend;
my busy person, pearl of all our house;
my loved one, lover, scolder, all my own:
my blessed one – blessed centre of my home.

THE HILL BY MOONLIGHT

The fleeting earth is wild and sad,
and nightly does the moon abound,
and daily does the sun go round,
and, laughing at eternity,
reflects both day and night for me.

I sit and listen to the sound
of music in the trees.
This hill has much to say to me,
for she has long been here,

and as I sit and wait for her
the life within her belly stirs,
while the wind makes mention to the trees
of things that might have been.

Near to this hill I'll build a house –
of timber, slate and stone,
and some day at the foot of it
I'll lay down flesh and bone.

I wonder when the day shall come
when my few days are all but done,
shall I remember how and when
I sat and saw the fleeting earth
go sailing with the moon?

THE VALLEY

When I return to the lone hills
the valley has a woman's charms,
with half a dozen scattered farms
enclosed within her gentle arms.

For here is little life of man,
and on it he has made his mark,
and drawn his own kind picture here,
as if he'd smoothed her flowing hair,
and made her sing to his sweet song.

CONTRADICTIONS

How can laughter ring when no men happy are?
How can two people be so close and yet so far?
How can pleasure come from so much pain?
How can songs arise out of a tortured brain?

How can failure come out of so high a hope?
How can pain pursue so sweet a pleasure?
How can chaos be when all is in its place?
How can cruelty come from such a lovely face?

How can war go on, though all may wish it other?
How can love and hate be one with one another?

SOIL

On this day, the breathing earth
gave this little primrose birth.
On this day the living soil
yielded up its golden spoil.
Engaged in such a noble toil,
who despises simple soil?